POETRY
now

CELTIC CONNECTIONS 2003

Edited by

Heather Killingray

First published in Great Britain in 2003 by
POETRY NOW
Remus House,
Coltsfoot Drive,
Peterborough, PE2 9JX
Telephone (01733) 898101
Fax (01733) 313524

SB ISBN 1 84460 739 9

FOREWORD

Although we are a nation of poets we are accused of not reading poetry, or buying poetry books. After many years of listening to the incessant gripes of poetry publishers, I can only assume that the books they publish, in general, are books that most people do not want to read.

Poetry should not be obscure, introverted, and as cryptic as a crossword puzzle: it is the poet's duty to reach out and embrace the world.

The world owes the poet nothing and we should not be expected to dig and delve into a rambling discourse searching for some inner meaning.

The reason we write poetry (and almost all of us do) is because we want to communicate: an ideal; an idea; or a specific feeling. Poetry is as essential in communication, as a letter; a radio; a telephone, and the main criterion for selecting the poems in this anthology is very simple: they communicate.

CONTENTS

SHELTER

Years before I had kissed her here
On this very spot
And as the rain started to ease
I remembered so many things.
Looking up at the sky
I left my shelter,
It was a huge chestnut tree
That glistened in the rain.
Westward,
Huge cracks in the broken clouds
Let through a large, violent sunset.
Straight ahead the sky was dark slate
Untouched by the fire that melted the sky.
Every blade of grass and tree
Dripped with rain
And the road I travelled on,
Shone like a river.
The last drops of rain
Fell like gentle reminders.

Paul Willis

BENIGN ANGELS - DUNKELD CATHEDRAL

The hidden wolf sleeps
Behind the altar

Eaten by worms in death
As he destroyed in life

Under the heavenly gaze
Of benign angels

Carved in oak
By unknown hands

Years since.

R H Rodger

THE BLACK TIE GUYS

When people pass away you'll always hear someone say,
It was sad, but it does make you think,
If he'd listened to friends with whom time he did spend,
He should have maybe given up on the drink.

Another will go, the same people show,
This time they take a different tack,
I knew this guy well and to him I would tell,
What would kill him were the things in the pack.

Then another goes down, the clique stand around,
And wonder why they were not told,
About a healthy young guy who'll now never know why,
His heart suddenly then became cold.

We all know their faces, they visit different places,
For the grub, they're all at the venue,
They lay sympathy deep, then take a back seat,
And question, 'How come there's nae steak pie on the menu?'

John Boyle Weatherall

THE FAMILY TREE

My mother's love
poured forth on me
unreserved
given free.

Thus enriched
throughout my life
enabled me
to be a loving wife.

Time passed by
I had a son
my love poured forth
on the little one.

Grandchildren now
love filters through
unreserved
tender and new.

Family love
is a precious thing
draw deep from the well
of the eternal spring.

Myra D Walker

ALONE

Why do I feel alone
In a crowded room?
I feel so alone,
It sometimes makes me cry.
I want to get away
From this feeling that I have,
As it hurts so bad.
Maybe if it goes away,
I will not feel any pain.

Tracy Karen Neil

ENSURING, A LIE BELIEVED

Is there any way at all
To stop myself falling
To a place I don't want to be

I don't want to depend on you
I can't have you be all that I am
Because I know that you still love her

So I'd rather not know
Just how good we could be together
I'll just have to live with the 'if only'

But each time I see you
My heart's torn in two
Haunting me that you could be the one

But I can't surrender to temptation
I choose not to travel
A path that can only lead to pain

So I'll decide to lie
Say that I have no feelings for you
Regretting the very moment for evermore.

Elaine Donaldson

FOREVER

An eye for an eye, a life for a life,
A husband for a husband, a wife for a wife,
Give me your heart and I will treat it like a crown,
Always stand by you and never let you down.
Give me your soul and I will treat it like a jewel,
Will make sure you're not a fool.
Give me your life and that's something I will treasure
And promise to love you forever.
If I give you my heart will you do the same,
Hold your head high and never be ashamed?
If I give you my soul will you guard the lot
Or leave it behind like something you've forgot?
If I give you my life keep it safe in a locket
And wherever you go carry me in your pocket.

Michelle Birch

MUM

I look at all that's beautiful,
I search through verse and fable,
But naught compares I've seen nor heard . . .

You're awesome,
You're ineffable.

Deirdre Dewar

THE FOUNDATION

Far gone is the summer,
lost among the cloud,
nature cringes in silence
as distant thunder roars aloud.

Dull sky opens up,
rain comes pouring down,
flowers droop their heads,
leaves turn a dirty brown.

Wind becomes colder,
sleet begins to fall,
ice forms on puddles,
hedgerow cowers behind the wall.

Snow covers rooftops,
fields are brilliant white,
winter has laid the foundation
to make the dark evenings bright.

Zakk Reid

THE MOVE

Moving day is here at last.
It is a gradual process,
Not one that goes fast.

It is extremely time consuming and
Patience is required, but
If things are properly organised,
One will end up a bit less tired.

One has a good clear out and
Has to be ruthless,
There are essential things to keep
And those that are useless.

Charity shops are certainly handy.
There, customers will find
Discarded goods quite dandy.

Unpacking fortunately doesn't take so long,
Provided the boxes have been quite strong.
Trust that nothing is broken
As there is enough to do,
Without having to resort
To using super glue!

Eventually one can relax and
Enjoy the home they've chosen.
They can surely be forgiven,
Should they only feel like dozing!

Joan C Igesund

HOTEL FIRE

The fire bell rang with a strident clang
And he leapt up out of his bed,

He ran to his door on the fifteenth floor
And opened it with dread.

From the stairs below came a flickering glow
Of flames leaping, yellow and red.

He stood in a dither not knowing whither
He should have turned and fled.

Had he run to the right he'd have found the flight
Which to safety would have led;

But he couldn't remember and was burnt to an ember,
Round and cosy and red.

He ran to the left and left a family bereft
With hearts which wept and bled.

He ended up cremated, rather early, not belated,
When he'd planned to be interred instead.

This sad and sorry tale has a moral to avail
For every Tom, Dick and Fred -

On the back of every door on each and every floor
Read the info which is spread

So you won't expire in a hotel fire
And end up prematurely dead.

Myrna R Forrester

RESPITE

We are drifting into darkness
And it flows smooth and inky
Into our mouths, across our eyes
And through the scribbled scratches of this day.
All my Heaven, all my Hell
Is measured ounce for ounce
In your warm weight upon me
And there is silence falling here.
I do not have to speak.
You do not have to listen.
It is this time of precious nothing
I will grieve for when you leave.

Suzanne Kennelly

BORN AND BRED

My land is evergreen
With mountains proud and high
And lochs deep and clear
That mirror stars and sky.

I see beauty in each sunrise
While poetry floats on the breeze
And sweet Celtic music plays
From the rivers to the seas.

The stag stands silent and still
'Gainst the skyline set ablaze
And amidst the purple heather
Enthralled I stand and gaze.

But of all the things seen and done
It does have to be said
That the people are the treasure
Of our nation - Scots born and bred!

M M Graham & Mary A Shovlin

IONA

Iona
an island
a special place
and the sun delivers
light and shade
ebbing flowing
always
caressing cliffs
that wrap around
jagged coast hidden caves
protecting the core
spiritual home
Iona

Bryan Beattie

SONG FOR MURDER

And the rain came down over us.
And we did not know from where.
And no one knew from where.
And the bracken bent.
And the earth clogged with filmy tears.

And the people stood, empty eyed
In the cornfields, in the schoolhouse
In the airbase.
They asked with pale faces,
In the skies and the riverbanks,
As they caved in.
They asked, with their heads receding into grief,
With their hands which were no longer hands, legs
Which were no longer legs, but unfamiliar
Flanges, useless and unsupporting.
They asked one another in the trembling,
And the sickness of the daylight,

And Scotland felt
Like a stomach turning over into mud.

Ruth Barker

SUNSET

Solemnly he sinks into the desolate horizon.
And with his final breath he dusts the heavens,
With his golden rays,
Leaving his passionate warm colours,
To penetrate deep in the skin,
And to stain the soul with regretful hope.
While the leaves tremble in his departure.

Cautiously the night seeps in boldly.
Destroying the silken sky.
Quickly comfort drains away form the face,
And worries thunder the mind.

So envious is the night.
He quickly draws cold darkness tightly,
Around the land.
Whilst soft wings of silence spread infectiously,
Pouring into innocent ears.
While the leaves remain stationary.
Drenched in fear.

Pauline Hall Barrientos (17)

NOTHING

The sun that slowly soothed my summer heartache
Has faded away,
What now shall I call my saviour?
Loneliness speaks my name, yet I feel abundantly full
Of, nothing.
What earthly ship shall carry me away
Into the great sea of peacefulness?
No man or material substance can fill my empty soul.
I will go into my voyage of life unreluctantly so,
So full of, nothing.
Unfull,
Unsatisfied,
Unresolved,
But overcome,
With nothing.

Colette Rose Rushton

WE ARE ALL TRAVELLERS

The road from here to there seems long.
Before we leave, we pack
whate'er we think we'll need.
And halfway there we break our journey.
Sitting in a village graveyard
by the sea,
that other journey comes to mind.
The one we all must make.
No packing to do.
No route to plan.
No cases, bags or tickets.
The only box we need,
the one we're in.
This trip takes no time.
Now we are here.
Then we are there.
No distance,
no time.
Just passing over.

John J Lafferty

LOCH GARBAD

Fir trees and heather
Embrace the tranquil lake and blush
With a purple glow.

Asja Baumgärtner

ST GILES, EDINBURGH

I was there, next to the pigeoned monument
in front of St Giles at the time we arranged.
I watched the large, pale hats of a wedding
mushroom in the entrance, scanned the tour groups
for your beard. A minstrel, emerald green and red,
shook the bells of his three-cornered head-dress
at a child, grinned, and struck up a Beatles medley
while the photographer's tripod pranced on the steps
of the cathedral, and foreigners snapped Scotland:
the bride; the Rolls; men in kilts lighting cigarettes.

When you didn't come, I looked for another entrance
round the side, searched the spiked wig of scaffolding.
'Scotland the Brave' brought me back to the monument,
but the piper stopped to scratch his knee and check
his watch, and his instrument lost its breath and died,
while the minstrel's electric guitar gently wept.

Sue Vickerman

UNTITLED

it's difficult to write poetry
so often it goes wrong
for people who deserve better

it's also difficult to commit suicide
to climb to the peak of the mountain
reach out to the furthest boundary of yourself
and not break
and in that space
to create all that you can
in anguish
in prayer
in love
sometimes I'm just brave enough
to try
to write.

Basia Palka

CULLODEN MOOR

(16th April 1746)

Go stand and stare on Culloden Moor, if you can on a fine
summer's day,
Listen to the sounds of birdsong, watch falcons soaring in the air.
As you look out over the moor, I'm sure if you strain your ear,
Far away off in the distance, ethereal silences you can hear.

An atmosphere of the spiritual slowly wraps itself quietly around,
Although others may not be near you, there is a sombre, mystical sound.

If you consider the death and destruction, that had occurred on its
barren face;
On this elevated expanse of moorland, the Jacobite rebellion
had taken place.

Prince Charles Edward Stuart, the Young Pretender as he was known
Tried and failed to depose George II to capture the British throne.
The Scottish Highland army, lost in excess of one thousand brave men,
In comparison to less than the three hundred of British troops who
met their end.

I cannot imagine the bloody murder and mayhem
That was meted out on that dreadful night,
The screaming, the moaning, the anger,
Surely must have been an horrendous sight.

As in a trance I look over this battlefield, feel the tormented spirits
move around me,
No words can explain my emotions, having never experienced
such feelings you see.

If you ever go to north east Scotland, especially the Highland
capital of Inverness;
Known locally as the Drummoisie Muir, a tract of land of
particular wildness
Should you go and pay your respects on what is a burial and battlefield,
I assure you when you leave, your sadness you will find hard
to conceal.

So take my advice and go visit where the last battle was fought on
Scottish soil,
Where the Scottish against the English army, tried in vain this
massacre to foil.

Margaret M Donnelly

TAKE MY HAND

This is my motherland,
The ground on which I stand;
Come, see such a grand sight,
Dear friend, it's Scotia's beauty and might;
Come, take my hand.

Mountains, shades ever new,
Rivers, though not a few,
Valleys in purple heath,
Waterfalls beside, above and beneath;
What wondrous view!

Come, see the forests high,
The reindeer, royal but shy,
Just smell the burning peat,
Sip the maltest dram, taste wild honey sweet,
Watch eagles fly.

Yes, it's my motherland
And, aye, its welcome's grand.
Come, make it your land too;
I am sure your blood's tartan, through and through.
Come, take my hand.

Ken Millar

FIELDS OF GREEN

Gone are my days of my childhood,
When in summer I ran free, across those
Many fields of green.
As I lay beside the winding, running brook,
I heard a corncrake call.
Alas these birds are hardly seen today.
Modern farm machinery
Has sadly got in their way.
Horses that once worked in golden fields
Of wheat or corn, they too are hardly used,
Except for museums, where
Old day farming is shown.
How I long to roam again
Across the land so wild and free.
Instead of green grass, houses and shops adorn,
Those many fields of green.

Maureen Connolly

REASON

Have you found the reason?
I've searched most everywhere.
Why is there no reason?
Most people just don't care.

We all accept too easily
What other people say.
We never stop to question
The picture they portray.

The cover of a book, it's said,
Cannot be judged, until you've read
The contents there that lie within,
And only then can you begin
To understand that cover binding.
Mysteries will start unwinding.

Jacqueline Given

LOUGHINISLAND

Lapping up the sunshine
On a bright and warm sunny day.
Dandering through Loughinisland
With the hawthorn blooming in May.

The fields are many behind me
With hedgerows in between
The view it is so wonderful
The best I've ever seen.

The Mourne Mountains in the distance
That sweep down to the Irish Sea
Little country cottages
With wild flowers growing free.

For miles you can see the greenery
Of Ireland's beautiful ground
The hills and the meadows
In Loughinisland they surround.

The tranquillity and the peacefulness
An odd blackbird sings his song
The sheep in the far off fields
I see as I stroll along.

This is the place of contentment
And beauty beyond all means
Not enough is known, about Loughinisland
And its picturesque scene.

Geraldine McMullan Doherty

SUNLIGHT

Before you, there was no trust.
I had felt the darkness crowd in.
I dreamt of reaching out for your hand,
Of taking me back into sunlight.
I had let sadness and anger dominate me.
Bitter, afraid and standing on a knife edge,
Then like a flower to the sun I turned to you.
Whilst others made me weep
And drove me to the ground,
You stood by me and gave only happiness.
When I was weak, you shared your strength,
And when I hurt you, you forgave.
But please remember when you turn your back to leave,
Flowers always need a little sunlight in their lives.

Racheal Hamilton

TIME

Time on silken threads controls our destiny
It is the golden glow in our souls
Much too precious to waste
Time is for loving, giving and sharing
So much time for a baby
So little time for old age.
Thinking of the time to come
Looking back at time gone,
Regrets or none at all.
Time gives us new experiences
But only if we listen and learn.
Time cannot be held in our hands
Only on gossamer wings in our heart.
It is like a big silver moon
Gleaming, shining, always there.
Without time, we don't exist.

Anne Boyd

THE VILLAGE OF SIXMILECROSS

Sixmilecross, unique and tranquil
Resting in the Sperrins' arms
Captivating beauty uncomprehended
Oblivious to explorers and tourists' demands

Sixmilecross with fertile farmland
Fields of maze grow proud and tall
Clothing fields with golden splendour
Fringed with rivers and waterfalls

Hidden treasure in stone-built structure
Church built in the famine years
Reminder of times when folks had little
But loneliness and silent tears

The hiring fair evoked much sadness
A widow parting with her child
Wages small though it meant survival
Few had respect for the orphan child

Old school house displays stone-build structure
Heritage of W F Marshall Baird of Tyrone
Sixmilecross quaint rural village
Historical epitaph
Marks centre of Tyrone
Tyrone among the bushes.

Frances Gibson

EXODUS

In the echo of the Lambeg drum
The sound of their footsteps
Running away
The glare of the orange
Reflected on green
Grassy verges
Hidden beneath
Weary feet

Brains too tired to walk
To war
Lay plans
Escape
Exodus

Grand Master, leading
Parting the green seas
Our taxes
Taxi them
Escort the exodus

We pay
For their footsteps
And follow away
A way away
From the stamping
Tramping March onwards

Out of this Egyptian July isle
We wander, driven
To our Israel
No eleventh night - no eleventh hour
Escape, exodus.

Chelley McLear

STONES OF IRELAND

Stones of ancient memories
Rise in Atlantic form
To gently wink at the troubled sky
Where rain clouds dance away
The heartaches
Of a history screaming for peace

North-west waves splash
Hoping to corrode
And wear away the secrets
Of a hidden past,
Where giants dreamed their hopes
And gave their minds a chance to wander
Like stones with magical voice

A windy chill rings fast
With a whistle in its tone.
The haunting voice of Finn MaCool
Echoes around each shapely stone
For the Causeway coast is his
And his alone.

Keith Henderson

CRACK OF DAWN

I woke at the crack of dawn
To hear the birds chirping on the window sill
And the coldness of the winter morning
Embedded in my skin as I rose from the bed.

Running to the hot press
I opened the door and stooped inside,
For the warmth was so inviting
I wanted to close the door and stay.

I got dressed at the hot press door
Then walked four or five paces to the bathroom.
There, the warm water from the hot tap
Was a godsend on my cold flesh face.

I could hear the wind blowing wildly outside
From the window at the top of the landing.
It was one of those mornings that make you wish
You had stayed in the warmth and comfort of your bed.

Downstairs I put on the teapot
And toasted bread under the grill,
As the hot tea and toast
Would insulate me against the cold outside.

Neely McGinley

WHEN YOU LOVE SOMEONE

If the days are getting colder
And the road, it has no end.
If there's something you love
On it you can depend.
If the nights are getting wetter
And all you do is cry,
Think of the way things used to be
And you will wonder why!
If things worked out the way you planned
And people treat you good
Just hold your smile and start again
And lighten up your mood.

If there's something you love
Let go and set it free
Judge the love by the time it takes
To come back or to flee.
When you love someone
It's like you can fly,
Swim through the clouds
And into the sky.
It's like you can hold them
And not let them go
Like a candle burning brightly
Amongst the cold, cold, snow.

But when the love is over
And the candle is still bright
Resolve yourself and try again
Reclaim your spot in light,
But if the candle burns right down
The feelings and love are gone,
For there the ashes lightly lay
Where that gleaming candle shone.

Blow the ashes far, away
Towards the shining sun,
For you to come back for love again,
When you love someone.

Judith Doherty

SEPTEMBER FACE REMEMBERED

A year ago September
two strangers briefly met
joked, laughed, talked awhile
that day was wet;
yet it's her smile
that I still remember.

I can't say why
that look so rare
recurs then lingers new
in my thoughts. Care
flees, sorrows are few
one year's gone by.

Eleven months, thirty days
mindful of her glance
I watch with pain
waiting for one chance
of meeting her again
passing along my ways.

Waiting; looking for some
sign of her. Last
year it rained. Wet
streets anew today. Past,
present, pause. I fret
anxious. Will she come?

Anthony J Brady

DARLING MAN

Darling, I love you, I really, really do
and I always want to be with you
through the good times and the bad,
I never want to see you sad.
I love the way you touch me,
I love the way you feel,
I love the way you kiss me,
I love the way you dance,
the world can feel our romance.
You have wonderful hands,
a charming face
that no one on Earth can replace,
because you are my darling man.
I'm going to do the best I can
to keep you near, my darling dear.
So now you know the way I feel,
I seal these words with a loving kiss,
so my love you cannot miss
my beautiful, darling man.

Carol Mary Woods

THE PARTING

Softly shining the sun touched the hilltop,
Slowly falling it cast shadows around us,
I felt his hand as it reached for mine,
And we watched our reflections in the lake.

As the clear sky began to fill with stars,
The people left the park but we remained.
No conversation, yet mutual understanding,
As we sat together on the river bank.

Time passed slowly but there was so little time,
We could feel the end closing in on us but we couldn't speak.
So much to say and so little time,
As the sun disappeared behind the hilltop.

And still I remember how we parted,
A single kiss then the good times vanished.
He smiled as he walked away and I was alone,
And the moon and the stars shone brightly in the sky.

Marion Quinn

MEMORY

He stood and gazed.
And seen the promised land
And seen that many had fallen.
For what?
And yet the silent sound of
Hope, memory and love
Filled his heart
People house a long memory.

M Trainor

UNTITLED

Night came with kisses goodnight and warm tender dreams
morning came with just a sign
visits were made from week to week
just to be told I was an over-protective parent
non-stop pushing I was finally heard.

Tests are done only to be told the war has finally begun
the terrorists are out doing their job
their primary subject hiding in places unknown
operations go ahead and drug warfare begins
months go by and you told us to go home, all looks well.

Eight-weekly assessments, a quick glance and no tests
pushed aside as if you don't exist
a year passes, something strange,
you know deep down the war is still on
the terrorists continue, the primary subject not found
'You are disabled, maybe it's a blessing,'
little do they know a blessing it is not.

Drug warfare begins, ravages the body
and makes you feel weak
but the spirit fights on
another soldier dies at what cost.

Thousands were spent on the London Eye
when thousands could be spent on the right equipment
to pay for caring and genuine staff
to fund the primary subject
before his terrorists start
to keep families together and
beat this war we call cancer.

Tina McAuley

DYING TREASURES

One night in October on a lonely Boston Street
I found an old man dying so I knelt down by his feet.
When I phoned in about this mugging I heard the old man say,
'Please hold my hand and listen to what I have to say.

They've gone and stole my wallet, my gold and plastics too,
But the thing I treasure most of all - I'm gonna give to you.'
He would not heed my protests but gripped tight upon my hand
And began to share his memories of his beautiful homeland!

'I was born in Northern Ireland so far across the foam
And Tyrone is the county that I think of as my home.
Now promise me that you'll take me there when I have passed away
And lay my bones where I can see the mist upon Lough Neagh.'

His words transported me across the sea to a place called County Down
Where St Patrick he was laid to rest in old Downpatrick's town,
Then up towards the Causeway and along the Antrim coast -
And felt myself transported as he continued with his boast!

We travelled round the coastline 'til we came to the Derry walls
Then his voice was slowly fading as he said, 'I hear the banshee calls -
But first let's see Fermanagh with her lakes so bright and blue
That stretch the miles from Rosslea, Derrygonnelly and Belcoo.

'There's one more treasure you must have if you're to have them all
And that's the Armagh County from Richill to Loughgall.'
And with his dying breath he said, 'Take me down through Gortin Glen
And we both will have the pleasure of returning home again!'

Now, I have come to Ireland with that old man's ashes in an urn
And I have kept his dying wish that to Ireland he'd return,
And I came and claimed those treasures that he had given to me
'Cos I've settled here in Ireland instead of far across the sea!

Cora-E Barras

My Supernatural Lifeline

I call out in the darkness
When my faith is growing weak.
On sunbathed days I praise You
But still, Your counsel seek.
Through every chapter of my life,
Your steadfast love has shown.
You speak into my very heart,
When I would feel alone.
The quiet times I share with You
Cut through the shapeless gloom.
Your words provide a guiding light
In which my hope can bloom.
Every day can feel a struggle,
But when I speak to You
My load is lifted from my shoulders,
My spirit stirs anew.
In the haze of every broken day,
When I'm crawling on the ground,
Or joyful days when my heart is singing,
Your presence can be found.
Rain or shine, You never leave
Instead you stand close by.
Rejoicing in my happy times,
Crying when I cry.
You are my Lord and Saviour,
My friend, my rock, my light,
My supernatural lifeline,
The sun that ends my night.

Sarah Louise Pedwell

LOST CULTURE

Remember Penyberth and Saunders Lewis
Remember Tryweryn a valley drowned
Wales is dying
Another notch in the imperial crown
And English prince in '69
A culture fading that should be yours and mine
Remember Merthyr, Rebecca, what can be done
Remember the prince and the betrayal at Caernarfon
The country is dying
The mines have gone
The slag heaps remain
Remain in our memory.
Remember Glyndwr
The last prince of Wales
What price for freedom
And democratic rights
Wales is fading out of sight.
Remember the language
Remember the pits
Destroyed by governments that couldn't give a s***
Remember the farms and holiday homes
Robbed of language and culture
That I've never really owned.

John Houghton

ALEXANDRA PARK

An enchanted space so full of
Joy
On a hill
Overlooking
The
Glittering sea.
Sun streams through the aged trees
And
Gossamer fairies
Dance
In wooded glades.
Squirrels
Spring
From branch to branch
And
Wild birds
Sip
From
The silvery pond
And children
Skip
On the
Lush green velvet
Whilst
Flowers
Bask
In their
Beauty.
And
All is well.
And
All is safe.

Acknowledging
Perfection
In this
Tranquil
Sacred
Place.

Judith M Veal

Judith .M. Veal .
Dedicated to all who
love me & who I
adore . ♡ ♡

BURN ME

I don't know who I am anymore, this is something I can't avoid
Pull me up off the ledge and watch me fall into the void
I've been here too long, I'm sick of playing this game
Hold my hand and walk with me as I walk into the flames
I can dream when I close my eyes, look at me when I'm scared
You look like a Devil child when you're standing there
I surrender to suffering with my pain, cut away the emptiness inside
The rotting heart and hollow core I see when I look inside

I wish you could be here to watch me fail
Don't put the flowers on my grave
I'm walking up towards the fire
Watch me burn as the flames get higher.

Jonathan Jones

THE SCHOOL BELL

It's monumental, cold,
'Hold it like this,' the man says,
his hand dumbs the clapper.
She wants to ring the bell,
shake the handle,
make the sound resonate.
'At playtime,' he says.

It seems an eternity.
She is dealt a large sheet of paper
and a jam jar of water,
smells the bright paint.
The clock tells time,
pictures in a circle.
She doesn't know what it says.

She plays with the brush,
it doesn't satisfy.
She moves colours across the paper,
paint drips like street lights.
She looks at the clock,
'Is it time yet?' she asks.
'Soon,' he says.

She swirls her brush in dirty water,
plays with the jar and the bristles.
She wants, she wants.
At last -
'Now,' he says, handing her the bell.
She shakes the handle,
scatters sound like seed.

Sue Moules

WATER

As I stand on the shore enrapt
The waves loll up and down the beach.
The shale is thrown by the water and shushes the sea
But deaf water marches on to find the moon.

I step back leaving a crater in the wash
Too soon obliterated by the tide.
White horses dance a victory dance
Then collapse, exhausted, on the shore.

A girl lowers her bucket in the brine
To capture a moat for her castle.
Soon the water will return through the sand
As will I, pulled back by the beating of the tide.

Abigail Phillips

WALKING OUT IN ABERYSTWYTH

We decide to walk as evening approaches
and arrive at the bay, to find it dressed for the occasion
with a strand of sparkling Tiffany beads.
Behind us, touched up and tacky with white gloss
the terrace is in season
and through glazed sea views
the residents nod in silvery unison.
Forgetting - remembering,
where they went, today.

'Come to the edge,' I say,
and we stand watching the cream sea foam
curdle and rattle over the pebbles.
Feeling the damp chill breath of the waves,
measuring the moment.
Another year, ebbing and flowing.
A second chance.
Without reservation, we close together,
marvelling at our escape.

Celia Saywell

GUIDANCE PLEASE

Who can I turn to?
I know what my mind and body will go through.
An unwanted pair of shoes, take them back to the shop,
A wanted pair of shoes, easy, make a swap.
An unwanted or wanted pregnancy,
Who can I turn to?
Shall I put myself in the hands of the Baby Thief
While the infant is growing inside me?
Do not shun me, or shout at me.
Dear Lord, I know not what to do.
Who can I turn to?
I did not use my foolish head
As I laid beside you in your bed,
Now I must question my heart,
Should I, or should I not part
With this baby who is growing inside me?
If I have you little boy or girl,
A sister or brother for the child I have now,
My head will be in a whirl.
If I do not have you, I shall be bereaved,
Mourning for someone I do not know,
But I must know you, my dear, dear, child,
Because you are a constant reminder,
You're growing inside - inside my body.
Mary gave birth in a stable,
This is no fable,
And this is why I can say, today,
Dear Lord, I know what to do.
Love me, guide me, and lead me through,
Lead me through the next nine months,
Until I give birth to my child.

I listened to you Lord,
I did not go to the Baby Thief,
Thank you for being by my side
And please guide those poor women
Who have no choice
But to part with the nameless child.

Miriam McKay

WAR BY NEWSFLASH

It's entertainment, someone said, not war,
A gentle evening ramble round the dead,
Complete with burnt-out trucks and tanks
To make a backdrop for the newsman's head.

With images and maps computer drawn
The anchorman sums up the battle lines
And cuts to army spokesmen holding court
At hourly briefings safe from deadly mines.

Recalling blackout and austerity
We wonder at the blazing city lights,
Forgetting that the cameraman needs power
To bring onto our screens these wartime sights.

No need to foil attacks by keeping dark
When modern warfare seeks its targets blind,
So giving the reporter far more scope
To gently titillate the viewer's mind.

So, careless that the mounds of brick and stone
Were once a people's life that is no more,
The brooding battery of camera shots
Plays out the modern ratings game of war.

Phillipa Giles

DIGGING FOR MIASMS

Cambrian, Ordovician, Silurian,
The terrain
That lies beneath.
In the ancestral space
Of the permafrost,
A relic of lives past
Drips its form
Into a stalagmite present.

A fossil imprint
Spins you in its threads.
Forming,
Deforming,
Holding you in the stranglehold
Of its stasis.

Possibilities vibrate
With every breath.
The skein unwinds
As you become yourself.
An insect flies
From its amber prison
Into absolute freedom.

Bethan Rees Jones

A TAILOR'S WIDTH OF PRIDE

Grey and wet-headed, peering over
   the hem of the mountain,
   He rests His head in His hands,
elbows propped in the valley.
No need to meddle.
Not a fold to smooth or seam to straighten.
Catches of silver threads
   glittering along a plush of green.
Resplendent at His feet.
Flecked and woven with a sky full of sighs.
This robe of inspiration, of hymns, of chapel
adorned for adoration,
while at the edge of the west,
the round eye of the dragon closes
   into the red tears of the tide.

Anita Lind

WELSH MOUNTAIN PONIES

When I was a boy I saw the ponies drinking
Up where the pines are fur on the mountain's flank.
They stood to their girths in the crystal water;
Docile, they drank.

Under their glossy sides the water rippled
In widening rings of amber and gold.
Under my hesitant foot a dry stick snapped;
They turned, long ears erect and bold.

Startled, they whinnied, their brown eyes rolling in fury;
The water, churned by their hooves, rose above their knees.
Crashing, they jumped the bank and emerald thickets
And vanished into the trees.

But never again have I seen the proud, shy ponies,
No mark of a hoof, or a crested head.
The woods and heights are bare,
The wild mountain ponies have fled.

Alan Hougardy

THE WARMTH OF HEAVEN

For a while, I've been watching the sun,
Falling behind the horizon.
With no clouds in the sky, to feed my imagination.
For this letter I'm writing, there will be no reply.
Only questions, for the reasons why,
No answers to swear by or chances for goodbyes.

In Heaven can you see me slide,
In Heaven can you read what I write,
In Heaven, can you hear my prayers late at night.
In Heaven, will the stars shine on
My nude wings when you strap them on,
For the haven flight into your arms.
The womb of Heaven wrapped in your arms.

With your smile, I am watching the sun,
Rising above the horizon.
With no clouds in the sky, to cloud my imagination.
To this letter I'm reading, I don't need a reply,
Or answers to the questions why,
Only chances to swear by, no changes or goodbyes.

In Heaven can you see me glide,
In Heaven do you like what I write,
In Heaven, can you hear my whispers late at night.
In Heaven, the stars will shine on
My new wings when you strap them on,
For the haven flight into your arms.
The warmth of Heaven wrapped in your arms.

P J Kemp

SCATTY FRIEND

Did I ever tell you what a good friend you are to me,
The friend I always think about, but very rarely see,
So I thought I'd send you a little note to say I care for you,
I hope you're always safe and well in everything you do.
I know I'm absent-minded and a little self-absorbed,
But a friend you'll always have in me, you can rest assured.
However, this is due to lack of time I have, I'm sure you'll understand,
Children turn your life around and take the upper hand.
I'm sorry I don't see more of you my friend, but I think of you a lot,
I cherish every moment of the friendship that we've got.

Love, scatty friend.

Rachel Okell

THE KEY

This house of pain my soul, harbours your ship, your death,
Your memory will always flow, like the blood through my veins.

My thoughts are filled with yours, I feel you, I know you,
I will remember how it was, I know how it is.

My voice speaks your words, my heart feels your emotions.
My eyes see you, but you are not there.

I hear the words you speak, but your mouth no longer moves,
I feel you touch me, but where are you?

My soul is like a chest, where is the key?
I must release my tears, I have to let you go.

You have fallen from life, my tears fall from my eyes,
They sting my cheeks, but you no longer feel pain.

The flames burn my body, your body, your protection,
Your ashes scattered, no longer a part of you.

I must rest now, as you sleep peacefully,
The key is in my heart, where you will be forever.

Victoria Golding

UNTITLED
(To the woman I wrote this for. You know who you are . . .)

I used to pray for an angel to come down
And save me from falling
And now that you've found me, you light the way.
You've given me hope, life and love.
Each day with you is heaven-sent and I feel
So grateful to you, my beautiful angel.

My love, you are my angel and I
Fly on your wings every time we're together.
Every gaze from your eyes, every breath on my cheek,
Every touch from your hands, you save me and
I thank God for sending you to me.

Love me forever, my angel,
And I will love you until the end of time.

Laurence Richards

THE TORRENT WALK OR FAIRY PARADISE

Bubbling, bouncing, pouring, flowing,
Rushing on to reach the sea;
Rushing on but tranquillising,
Its deep still pools trapped, yet free.

Moss in green abundance, covers
Boulders, trunks and hollows grand,
It's bright, soft growth, lush all over,
Carpeting this fairyland.

Yes, I am sure that this has to be
Home, for all little people
Who filled our minds, when we were three,
So mystical and magical!

Can't you just see them dancing round,
In and out, o'er and under -
So very small, they'll not be found -
Many hideaways to plunder!

These little folk are all such gems,
Pixies and elves and fairies;
All this is paradise for them,
No need for garden shrubberies.

The Torrent Walk in all its length
Is wonder, peace and beauty,
The water's running force, its strength,
Abundant growth its bounty.

Janet Bowen

THERE IS A REASON

There is a reason
    for the way that you are.
The years of pain and hardship
    can take their toll
But teach one to see
    inside their soul
No matter how big or old you get
    and life can be a bind
The sheer joy and innocence
    of a child trapped in your mind
The years of hardship
    sorrow and pain
If I met you again tomorrow
    I'd do it all again.

You have a way about you
    that teaches one to see
There is a reason
    why you were sent to me.

Carole Croney

HISTORY

'Have you read 'Mein Kampf'?' the jester asked.
Jesters all, we all thought it hilarious
That a monorchial (so they said, wrongly) and awkward-seeming
Ranter, with pretensions to 'art' and Wagner
Should scare *us!* (Sefton Delmer reported).

When did the brewing begin?
Was it with beer and lederhosen
In a Munich bierhof with some pals?

No. Remember the first World War?
(We called it 'Great' - the great mistake, maybe?)
After, the nations that 'won' acted bizarrely,
And 'Frenchly forced', forced the defeated lower still.

Oh yes, there was a 'red menace' even then;
But as though ourselves gassed with some idiocy,
Let the blind lead us, blind as we were,
Yet knowing, as Knut had known, that tide comes in
Eternally.

Thus, inevitable as tides,
All else unfolds:
'A tale told by an idiot,
. . . signifying . . . nothing?'

Geraint Jenkins

THE EDGE

I live on the edge of the country
I can almost fall off
Almost fall into the sea.
Sometimes I climb up high
Where purple foxgloves
Make an ugly bruise
On the shoulder of the cliff.
I live on the edge.

I live on the edge of my art
I can almost fall off
Almost fall into obscurity.
But sometimes I am fortunate
To find some neglected corner
In the human heart or mind
That I can make my own.
I live on the edge.

I live on the edge of love
I can almost fall in, hopelessly.
Sometimes I forget the racing years
And still stand strained on tiptoe
Eager to catch the rhythmic bird of time
Before it flies away
To wade in cold Welsh streams.
I live on the edge.

Rhoda Hodes

MEMORIES OF A SUMMER'S DAY AT BARRY ISLAND

A citrus sun sizzles high in an infinite sapphire sky over Barry Island
Toasting torsos doze on deckchairs scattered along the beach
Children sit on comforting sand, grabbing handfuls and letting it sift
through playful fingers.

Gentle rippling waves seep up the beach as the tide teases the toes
of nervous would-be bathers
Donkeys saunter across the sand, pulling their passengers in rickety
carriages and challenging elated children to lick lollies

Across the sparkling sea, a ship sails to tropical islands; children wave
energetically as it dissolves into the horizon
Alluring aromas of vinegar-soaked fish and chips, tease the appetites of
hungry holidaymakers
Coloured candy rock and cheeky postcards are bought by the handful
for friends and relatives missing all the fun

The soft warm breeze carries the sound of screaming thrill-seekers at
the funfair
Rapturous applauds accompany the sound of clinking coins as tourists
reap the rewards of hours spent playing penny machines

Soothing summer air begins to cool as the day passes its finest
Mothers beckon their children as they contently prepare to head home
Tourists reluctantly trickle away as the sun metamorphosises into a
burnt orange orb, descending the azure sky

As darkness advances, bright lights adorn the empty promenade, which
shines like 'Pearly Kings and Queens'
Contented and drowsy from the sun's calming effect, the remaining few
people wander home to welcome sleep, and to dream of another
summer's day at Barry Island.

Amanda Mayne

LONELINESS
(Dedicated to Nan)

Lonely I stand - isolated
The 'whirr' of life stampedes about me.
Intrusion seems hard, as my mind I sealed
As to my own carapace -
I'm an alien, an anomaly to all but me.
I can't stop feeling low.
If only there was an understanding
That I have in my soul
The reasons for my wastedness
Would soon to me be known.

Matthew McDonald (14)

SONNET BEFORE 4

I rose each day at four, before cockcrow,
Your will and bidding was my guiding voice,
Sunrise to set, was when I had to show
I was your servant and I had no choice.
The sun, the rain, the wind gave me a look
Which said that I belonged to a rare breed,
And those that looked on in envy, mistook
Me for someone who had it all indeed.
But then you changed and took away my pride,
Sold what I had to those who would not pay.
It was not just the animals that died,
A part of me as well, I'm sad to say.
Still worry not, who find this ode alarming,
Perhaps you've guessed, my love was farming.

Rick Taylor

PJ

PJ is dead
And there is a space where he used to be
Not in one place - but in many
In hearts and minds and farms and pubs
In country lanes where he used to trudge
Exhausted by his life
Feeling the wind and rain on his face
And sometimes the sun
Although not often in these parts.

The whisky bottles are all full now
And the fags unsmoked
And his wives and kids and friends
Stare in shock
At the hole in the ground where they are going to put him
So many people that most can't see
And have to file past like people in a museum
And the priest says nice things about a man named Peter
But not the man they knew
The rogue named PJ
Who played pool better than he danced
Cursed and broke your fingers in a fist that gripped regret
A man who broke his back for sixty years
Under cows and clods and mean men who paid him cash
A man with passion and a way with women
That led him down a labyrinth of lies
Until he lost himself in the bottle
A father and a mother to his many children
Most of whom he never saw in later years
And a fixture in the corner of the bar
Where all PJs sit.

Chris Sexton

HAIKU

Wet flowers of May
Bluebells drooping
Thirsty growth.

Jeni Roberts

WHEN I MET YOU

After a particularly boring night shift
When all I saw were drunks and taxis,
At 5 o'clock or thereabouts
A delivery van came into view
Carrying more than I could ever hope for.

After the driver came inside, a vision walked in
In a football coat and looking like
She'd just got out of bed
And bang! A lightning bolt, it could be said
(A cliché I know but what the hell)
Walked into my life and sweetly said,
'Do you mind if I have some milk?'

Well, from that moment at a glance
I knew my life would change
(Given half a chance)
I fell in love and from that day
I've been so happy (I must say).

From that day on we became great friends
And from that developed so much more
We laughed and joked, I watched in awe
At this beauty, wealth, it looks so poor
When I think of what I have today
I thank the stars for milk, for bread,
For my life this way.

Adrian King

WHY?

Rising sun
Gradually
Rolling up
Frost waiting
On the grass
Flowers yawn
Turn their heads
To the rays
Man rising
Cannot stop
Sun arcing
And shining
And warming
What's his role
In all this?

John M Sparkes

THE SWANSEA TRIP FOR CHRISTMAS

Let's pretend
it didn't end.
Let's have a day like that.
It's for the kids,
though you and I
know kidding ourselves
might get us by.
Just for today, let's live the lie.

Let's pretend
it's as we were.
So close, so caring.
So kind, so sharing.
Happy to be here-ing and there-ing.
Together,
Again,
Today.

Bryan Hackett

THE CROSS

How bright was the cross you gave me,
Plain and simple you said, like our love.
I wore it for my belief in you, not God
And it shone like our future.

Twenty years later it lies tarnished
And tangled in my drawer - the chain broken.
The only perfect link is 6ft tall and calls me Mam.

Dorinda McCann

RESTORATION
(September 1999, Kosovo rebuilding after the war)

Striving to raise the outstretched tree
Labourers pulled tangled branches free,
Some were severed and some were wedged,
Some were twisted and some were dead.
Their mighty task was at once confounded
By a myriad of onlookers who instantly surrounded,
Some were jubilant and some were tearful,
Some felt threatened and some were fearful.
Co-ordinated teams laboured on
Trying to control the frenzied throng,
Pushing and pulling the solid weight,
The tree they tried to reinstate.
With roots disturbed and branches broken,
Their concerted efforts were more than a token.
They harried and cajoled and sought to cope,
For many lived in desperate hope.
To restore a nation once again,
Would require much more
Than taking the strain.

Liam Heaney

MEN O' THE BLACK SEAM

When we turned eleven
our schooldays turned to memories.
The descent into the clanking dark
commenced as chalk-dust abandoned our nostrils.
Reborn as the men o' the black seam
when we turned eleven.

I cried myself to sleep at night,
bones stiffened in pain from cramp and cold,
inconsolable in fear of the hidden reaper
in the clanking dark.
The passage of time robbed me of my tears;
icy pain, a constant companion,
a nagging fishwife,
'till death us do part,
dulled down
as nerve endings died;
the fear of the hidden reaper,
blunted, suppressed.
I became a man, his childhood thieved
by the cut-purse hands of industry.
A man o' the black seam.

Down into the shaft with my father and friends,
this desperate camaraderie of the doomed enslaved.
We rode the squealing lift at the crack of dawn
into Hell's colon.
Wrestling nuggets of black gold from the earthen guts.
Belly-crawled through one foot of water
in two-foot high tunnels.
Hacked at Satan's visage 'til each muscle howled,
each sinew screamed.
Recoiled, blind panic at the putrescent rat's innards stench
of the ghostly whiff, the merest hint
of methane.

Then we went home the way we came.
In the dark.
In harmony.
Us men o' the black seam.
The saddest black-face minstrels
you ever did see . . .

Tony Bush

EXCUSES!

On the street of a thousand pot-holes
Past the vandalised dog and bone
There lurks an evil figure
Who never lurks alone.
For with it is a tiny mite,
A child, not like your own,
Who, if you let it come too close,
Emits a piteous groan.

So, on certain moonless nights,
Take, stranger, my advice:
Follow not the plaintive child
With eyes of pure cardice,
Sent forth, stranger, to entice man
Into the evil grasp
Of that foul fiend, who upon death weaned,
Will extract your last choked gasp.

Well guarded is that hooded ghoul
By hounds back form the dead;
The evidence is all around -
Especially where you tread!
And many roisterous revellers,
The odd one with a flagon,
Have seen this manifestation
And taken to the wagon!

So should you venture on this street
And hear the growls and snaps,
Ensure that you are well-prepared -
And wear your e-type daps!
Imagination, you may think, is running rather rife
But whene'er I come home late, it's what I tell the wife.

Gerry Rose

CONTENTMENT

Soothed by sunlight,
we lie under rippling leaves,
green as emeralds,
precious as these moments.

Life's stresses
sucked in by the sun,
its lingering fingers
massage beautifully.

Time slows to wisps of air,
an ebbing trail,
curling side by side,
trailing over us like fringes.

As two souls,
we beam our
thoughts and
feelings upwards,

like two stalks of light,
decorated by birds,
clustered and
dancing as flies.

Reflection
From sky's blue mirror,
one powerful
spark of ignited light

dazzles our eyes
and filters down us,
spilling as a puddle
of shimmering gold.

Jillian Shields

THEN IS THE WINTER

Then is the winter wind - blind in gullies:
a lion's head baptised
in the howling tin chapel time passing,
shaken fist days of numb roots,
cached in the hill curves,
that advance without let.

Where now the reason for reason?
No moonshells here, bundled in string;
but short-lighted:
mapped without legend
and not missed.

Not missed by the blackthorn
and trampling pools of the soft-eyed
stone-misted cattle;
hidden from shadows
by the stray fence: twinebound and nailed;
come to the day-locked door;
grown hidden by gnarlings
of slight honour;
with no footfalls now -
nor will be again.

Peter Jones

A LOVED ONE REMEMBERED

Darkness fell and we all knew,
that it was time to go.
We packed our things and said goodbye,
to the only life we knew.
What lies ahead a mystery;
what's gone behind a blur.
The only thing that's certain,
is that we'll never forget her.
For she was always there for us,
a rock to lean upon.
Now she's in our hearts forever
and there she will live on.

David Watters

FAILING TO BE

Thunder cracked the quiet hour,
Groaning the aching of the sky
Before tears fell down the glass.
I can't help but wonder why

It hurt with me. Tearing casually through
The quilt of stars as some great squawking
Bird of prey, her restless music
Arrives the moment silent talking

Keeps the hourglass turned again.
What seemed three was four,
But two was always one.
Thunder never brought one more.

David Russell

My Valley

The first stars were beginning to dot the sky
Glittering like a cluster of jewels
Against the dark shape of the mountains.
The lights of the valley below winking and beckoning
In an attempt to compete with them,
It was almost unbearably beautiful
And in the hush of a summer's evening
I stood on the mountain but my inward eye saw
Only the darkness of a valley once covered
With a shawl of blackness.
I heard the sound of colliery hooters,
And the tramp of miners' feet.
My heart was sad for the youthful dreams
Buried in the earth.
The stars will glitter in the sky for eternity,
The lights of the valley will be there for posterity,
And memories will stay in our hearts forever.

Phyllis Bowen

HOSTILE FORTS

Words are like birds;
they fly through the sky.

A word spoken here at first will be near
then it takes to the air and lands far over there
(. . . everywhere!).

This is the free nature of talk,
given wings by the ones who must walk.

And when we form our words to look like writing,
it's not the scribbled lines that are exciting;
it's how the scrawls express our minds' images
for others to make sense from senseless pages.

This language made from words helps you and I exchange our thoughts:
it joins us up as one like allies who communicate
and glide over the borderlines that else-wise separate
idea canaries in cages of body; friends . . . in hostile forts.

We can't climb in
each other's skin
to see the view,
so words
will have to do.

Carreg Sylwr

MY HIGHLAND HOME

How I loved my Highland home
with its surrounding heathered hills.
Where the only noise you ever heard
was from the foaming tumbling rills.

The deer grazed on the hillside slopes
their ears tuned to every sound.
Whenever they heard an alien noise
they were off in leaps and bounds.

The eagle swooped amongst the crags
searching for its meal.
If perhaps the hares were scarce
it was a lamb it had to steal.

I spotted an angler at a nearby loch
preparing to make his cast.
Hoping to make a victory
and nabbing a trout at last.

Those are the sights I saw most days
from my home amongst the hills.
This gave me lots of pleasure
and my heart with gladness filled.

Lachlan Taylor

EGYPT CAIRO

What shall I remember
On my return to my native land?
Will it be the blazing sun
Or yellow burning sand?

Maybe the cool of Alex
Compared to Cairo's heat
The natives so persistent
To rob you and to cheat.

These have gained impression
In my mind for future years
None can bring me rapture
As the thoughts of you somewhere.

When you and I my darling
Did part and say farewell
You took besides my heart
Treasures too great to sell.

Memories of nights we shared
Beneath the starry skies
The heavenly bliss of Egypt
And you my constant guide.

These things I will remember
Forever, so come what may
Always in the foreground
Time cannot dim them away.

Joan Prentice

THE NORWEGIAN CHURCH

It stands, a small, wooden, black and white church,
situated along the edge of the bay.
Shrouds of branches cling and protect it,
from the battering coastal winds which make it vulnerable.

It welcomes those who wish to enter, warmly,
to heavenly regions, rich with the promise of festive cheer.
A refuge for cold travellers from all nations and walks of life.
Locals, tourists, all those in need of a place to reflect
                                    and seek sanctuary.

As the early evening sky turns from fiery orange to the palest mauve,
some cold mortals can be seen, blurred and silhouetted in the dusk.
Undecided and unsure of their direction
seemingly bewitched by the sparkle and promise of dazzling lights
                                          across the bay.

They turn however, toward this building of worship and shelter
and taking in the simple, plainly lit Christmas tree outside,
Step inside the door to peace, hope and tranquillity,
as flickering lanterns highlight a rich, deep violet sky.

Mary Carroll

MEALS ON WHEELS

Fairies none at bottom of field,
Romany caravan shelters there
Thoughts of past life, gladden me
Wife, family gone, home no longer to share.

Caravan, home sweet home
'Old Ned's' clip clop
Between shafts, heard no more,
Places all known, wherever to go, stop!

Countryside fairs
Ply our trade
Sell our wares
Pegs, pans, lovingly hand-made.

'Neath birdsong, sun's smile
Sunrise, moon glow
Raindrops sparkling, flowers growing wild
Love songs ours, music to know.

Clean, polish brass
My pride joy
Daily task
Energy mine to employ.

Evenings, in quiet reverie
I smoke clay pipe
On van steps, soul at ease
Savour cuisine, meals on wheels, mine!

Ivy Lott

COMPOSURE

August silently stole the fragrance
from the long deep purple flowers
breathing heartfelt airs of summer perfume
in the still, warm night

standing spires of chivalry
knights moral characteristics
religious stems medieval and chivalrous
emblems defending insects of darkness

leaves crouching in despair
countenance for status composure
stars sparkling in lost heavens
as they reach towards untamed dreams

tortoises escaping unforeseen death
under astral counterplots
blossoms orange respectfully defending
their right to silence everlasting

Gina A Miller

MOODS OF THE SEA

The sea is so very calm today
a wild raging storm yesterday.
What will it be like tomorrow?
Will it bring joy or more sorrow?

The sea is also an angry place
for any mariner to have to face.
When sailing in a ship all alone
for fear of sinking like a stone.

The sea can be a very quiet place
where children can come to face,
the seashores lovely golden sand,
or to walk along, just hand in hand.

The mood of the sea always changes,
in far reaching and wide ranges,
from the smooth to the very rough.
To face it you have to be as tough.

John Harrold

THE SAME

People come and go here all the time
Nothing changes
I mean nothing to them
Wet and windy is May this year
Snow may come this winter
But it's still the same
The tears still flow
From being alone

Noel Thaddeus Lawler

JEWELS

*A mining company is to survey parts of the Hebrides and Scotland's
north-west coast to establish if they contain diamonds and sapphires
in sufficient quantities to be mined.*

Sunday Times report

Eden is gone and paradise is lost.
Torridon's twinned with Kimberley, Alligin with the Klondyke.
As for Lower Diabaig - it's San Francisco, 1849.

Shanties and wooden shacks will fill the scars
left by the brutal bulldozing of pines,
cedar and fir tree trampled underfoot;
slurry and slick and sludge pollute the bay,
coating the skin of seals, the tongues of guillemots;
the mountainside become a pit
with sullen mercenaries crawling up and down,
cursing in Greek or Portuguese;
the school a dosshouse, doubling as a saloon,
with powdered harpies reeking of gin and musk;
the manse a courtroom and the church a jail,
to take the residue left over from
the nightly shoot-out at the neon-lit
Och Aye Corral.

Is it inevitable or merely a condition of growing older
that changes in place and circumstance are always for the worst?

Why dig up paradise for bits of stone
when rubies hang thick upon the mountain ash
and egg-sized opals lurk amid lush emerald?
When pearls bedeck the cobwebs after rain
and diamonds on the surface of the loch
shimmer and shine, gleam in its crystal depths?

When gold enflames the sapphire of the sky,
turning to chalcedony and cornelian
and then to amethyst?

These things are certain.
May the survey fail.

Norman Bissett

THE SEA

A glorious day
It's Saturday
Where to go?

The beach maybe
Cool sea breeze
Salty air to breathe.

Golden grains
Softly massage
Tickling bare feet.

White gulls cry
Swoop and glide
Against the blue sky.

The crinkling surf
Curls and foams
Fingering the grains.

Ships on the horizon
Specks on the blue
Where sea meets sky.

The liquid sounds
Rolling in
And rolling out

Calming the mind
Letting go
A therapy.

Fuelling dreams
The ideal spot
It seems.

A glorious day
By the sea
Is the place to be.

Caroline C Hunter

THE WATER'S EDGE

I am by the tranquil water's edge
surveying swans glide disdainfully through
their noisy unruly cousins: the seagulls,
whose elegance as they fly low over the lake
counters the sound of their unseemly screams.
A swan with orange beak drifts close to shore,
as white as the majestic Scott Memorial
and in the warm spring weather of today
death in a frozen land seems an even sadder fate.
On the other side of the lake the opulent dwell
but their wealth does not protect them from
the petty problems which torment us all.

The dying daffodils now look forlorn,
a rustic tree stretches its fingers across the lake
and water reflects on to the sun-kissed branches
with shapes like snakes darting and dancing
like disco lights, the lake's movie screen.
I watch and find it hypnotic and mellifluous.

Then I observe an intricate spider's web
which the sun causes to glimmer,
a silver tightrope stretching from branch to branch.
The sun makes the lake shimmer
as if adorned with a myriad of dazzling stars
and as joggers perspire and elderly couples stroll
I allow the resplendent sun to soothe my soul.

Guy Fletcher

JUST FOR A DAY

If I had a wish for a day to be granted,
I can honestly say this is what I'd have wanted.
For twenty years my dad has long gone,
He got up one morning and died without warning.
I'd love to spend a whole day to amend,
By saying the things I should have said to him then.

The wonderful childhood I remember so well,
I danced on his feet, too small to keep up.
He was a giant - me a small pup,
We went to the pictures each Wednesday by bus,
I loved my special treat - Dad made a fuss.
Scrumptious sweets in a pretty dainty box,
I thought I was chocolate, a very posh toff.

Each year there were three very special days,
One of them Easter, my egg wrapped in bows
From Dad as ever, as pretty as a rose.
Then came my birthday, another great treat,
Something different each year, but always so sweet.
Last of all Christmas, all cosy and warm
A present again, I'd cuddle his arm.

Just for a day, if only I could,
To say as a loving daughter should.
Thank you Dad as ever before
Love you as always, for evermore.

B Thomas

RECAPTURED YOUTH

Whoever said that life was over
When you reach the big four-oh
Was mistaken!
For I am here to prove him wrong
To testify to that old maxim
That life begins at forty!

Lived the days of smelly nappies
Settling disputes of the offspring
PTAs and swimming lessons
Sat through dancing lessons' concerts
Checked the homework, did the washing
Thoroughly enjoyed it all.

Despite the worry and protection
Children lived, survived it all
And so did I!
Now they are so independent
Mother now has time to grow
To do all that she wanted to . . .

When she was young.

Opal Innsbruk

FOUR ON A BIKE

Just one bicycle, new and shining,
One whole mile to the village fair,
Four happy children set for adventure
But how the heck can they get there?
One on the saddle - it's his bike anyway -
One on the bar. Keep your legs stretched wide.
One on the carrier - not very comfortable -
No place left for the fourth to ride
What about the handlebars? Sit in the middle,
Be the navigator. The driver can't see.
All set! Off now straight down the school pitch
Faster and faster, four flying free.
Ooops! There's a hay cart coming towards us,
Turn to the right or we'll land in the hay.
Brake! Not the front one! Now we are airborne
Splash in the brook! No swingboats today.

Elizabeth Millington

REMEMBERING MY BEST FRIEND
(For Marie)

Go silently now,
Not looking how many people came.
Who remembered what this death was about,
Feel the atmosphere and emotions
That standing here will bring.
Lay aside the undertaker's form,
Declaring you were present,
Of course you would come
Tears and all.

We had laughed together,
She had been my confidante,
She had shared my secrets,
Known my first boyfriend,
Met him by the cemetery 'Kissing Gates'
And wondered what God would have thought!

Now her busy hands lie still,
Her wedding finger with wrinkled skin
Where once the gold had shone.
The ring she has left for me
To keep on shining
Through our golden memories of love . . .

Margarette Phillips

MY FAVOURITE SPOT

There's water as far as the eye can see
This is a favourite spot for me
The Atlantic Ocean round the Irish shore
On a private beach . . . Who could ask for more?
Just to wander barefoot on the sand
To witness all around . . . God's hand.
I lose all stress amid this peace
The worries of my life just cease.
Early morning is the best time of day
Before any people come this way.
The rocks, the mountains, ocean and sand
Are all so wonderful and grand.
This is the scene I call to mind
When I want to leave my troubles behind
I close my eyes and I can recall
This lovely spot in County Donegal.

Mary Anne Scott

A GARDENER'S NIGHTMARE

Birds in the garden are becoming a pest
When they wake in the morning
And are leaving the nest
They start getting people out of their beds
And hang around tweeting until they've been fed.

They peck all the seed heads
And grass you have sown
Make a mess of the gutters
And lawns freshly mown.

And when they have eaten
They will look for a drink
From downpipes and overflows
It just makes you think.

They have scattered chopped bark
All over the place
Took off in a hurry
Though not in disgrace.

They make holes in fresh earth
When looking for grubs
And not happy with that
They're attacking my tubs.

It takes so long to do them
And how my back aches
And I know it was them
Cos it hangs on their face.

So they've got one last chance
And if they ignore that
I'll just lose my temper
And get me a cat.

B Smith

SUBMISSIONS INVITED
SOMETHING FOR EVERYONE

POETRY NOW 2003 - Any subject,
any style, any time.

WOMENSWORDS 2003 - Strictly women,
have your say the female way!

STRONGWORDS 2003 - Warning!
Opinionated and have strong views.
(Not for the faint-hearted)

All poems no longer than 30 lines.
Always welcome! No fee!
Cash Prizes to be won!

Mark your envelope (eg *Poetry Now) 2003*
Send to:
Forward Press Ltd
Remus House, Coltsfoot Drive,
Peterborough, PE2 9JX

**OVER £10,000 POETRY PRIZES
TO BE WON!**

Judging will take place in October 2003